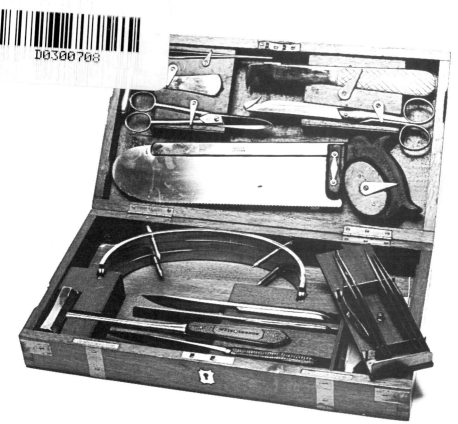

A comprehensive set of postmortem instruments in a brass-bound mahogany case. In the lid of the case are the spine wrench, bone chisel, bowel scissors, forceps, scissors and saw. In the base are the skull rest, mallet and knives, and in the lift-out tray further small scalpels.

OLD MEDICAL AND DENTAL INSTRUMENTS

David J. Warren

Shire Publications Ltd

CONTENTS

Published in 1999 by Shire Publications Ltd, Cromwell House, Church Street, Princes Risborough, Buckinghamshire HP27 9AA, UK. Website: www.shirebooks.co.uk

Copyright © 1994 by David J. Warren. First edition 1994; reprinted 1999. Shire Album 308. ISBN 0 7478 0257 2.

Printed in Great Britain by CIT Printing Services Ltd, Press Buildings, Merlins Bridge, Haverfordwest, Pembrokeshire SA61 1XF.

British Library Cataloguing in Publication Data: Warren, David. Old Medical and Dental Instruments. – (Shire Albums; No. 308). I. Title II. Series. 610.28. ISBN 0-7478-0257-2.

All the illustrations in this book have been supplied by the author.

Cover: *(Above) A mahogany-cased postmortem set, c.1860, showing saw, bowel scissors, mallet, knives and a blow pipe. (Below left) A brass breast pump, with cupping glass, c.1880. (Right) A brass ear trumpet with composition earpiece, c.1880.*

An ebony-framed dental mirror; an ebony trocar and cannula set, the silver cannula normally housed within the hollow handle; and a plated set of Southey's tubes, the four tiny cannulae housed within the handle.

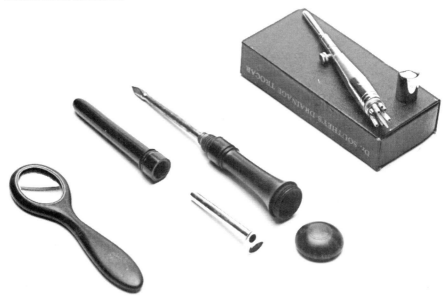

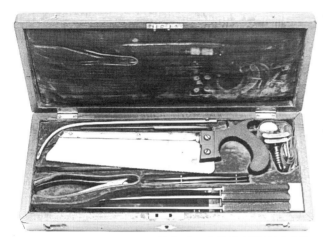

A mahogany-cased set of surgical instruments, c.1870, including a capital saw, urinary catheters, Petit's tourniquet, two scalpels with ebony handles, two large amputation knives and one catlin with hatched ebony handles, and rib forceps.

INTRODUCTION

Although large amputation instruments make a profound impact upon anyone who sees them for the first time, the range of medical antiques is much wider than surgical instruments. It extends from instruments used by physicians for diagnosis and treatment to infant feeders and the wide range of items found in the Victorian sickroom. It includes instruments for treatments now considered obsolete, such as bleeding and cupping, and the many items associated with diagnostic and therapeutic procedures whose validity has never been proved, such as phrenology and treatment with electro-galvanic devices.

Some collectors keep to their own field of personal medical practice, whilst others collect items made from specific materials, such as silver or ivory. The choice is vast, and in many collecting fields, such as invalid feeders or quackery, it is possible to assemble a representative group of items without great expense.

A ceramic pastille burner in the form of a cottage, c.1860; a blue and white invalid's spout cup, c.1840; a blue and white submarine-style infant feeder, c.1830; a blue and white pap boat, c.1840; a spout cup and a transitional pap boat, both showing the immortelle pattern, c.1920.

A cased set of ear, nose and throat examination instruments. Under the folded headband is the large circular mirror. To the left are a group of aural specula, at the top a set of long-handled mirrors and a tiny laryngeal brush, and the handles are on the right.

DIAGNOSTIC INSTRUMENTS

A large number of common complaints can be diagnosed, and many treated, by examination of the body cavities with a speculum. Specula are used not only to enlarge the view through, for example, the nose or rectum, but also, by virtue of their polished reflective surfaces, to improve illumination of the structures within the cavities such as the ear drum or the cervix. Instruments for this purpose have been made for thousands of years. Roman specula were found at Pompeii (AD 79), and specula were described by Albucasis in his tenth-century book on Arabic medical instruments.

Specula for the rectum and vagina tend to be cylindrical and many styles can be found, often named after their inventors. Some specula have a longitudinal split, so that the aperture can be adjusted, and Fergusson's speculum is of mirrored glass internally, to improve illumination. Specula with three or four blades, and a screw mechanism to adjust the aperture, have been known since Roman times, and many specula have removable wooden or ivory plugs to prevent injury during insertion. Specula for the nose and ears are often conical in shape and may be adjustable; sets of three or more may be found

Two vaginal specula: (left) with an ivory handle and three blades, adjustable by a hidden screw mechanism; (right) with ebony handle and two blades, with an adjustable screw stop.

in ear, nose and throat diagnostic sets.

Illumination was a problem common to all specula before the days of electricity. The Romans used silvered circular bronze 'speculum mirrors', which can still be found. In the eighteenth and nineteenth centuries a variety of means was used to achieve illumination, using candles, sunlight or oil lamps with a glass mirror.

Mouth gags are often included in diagnostic sets, to hold open the mouth, both to get a better view and to protect the physician! These may be of boxwood, ebony or steel, and some have mechanisms to adjust the opening.

Stethoscopes can be the subject of a whole collection, and many early styles can still be found. Before flexible tubing and the familiar 'binaural' stethoscopes were available, they were made of a single tube, with the physician's ear at one end and the patient's chest at the other. The first such monaural stethoscope, now rare, is the simple wooden cylinder described by Laennec in 1819. Later forms, still easily found, consist of a hollow tube, about 17 cm long, slightly flared at one end to form a cone to be applied to the patient's chest, and widened to form a flat disc about 6 cm in diameter at the

Below: *A rectal speculum in mirrored glass, with external gutta-percha covering, and a hole through which piles could be snared.*

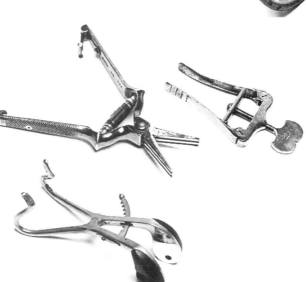

Above: *A cased set of three silver-plated Fergusson's vaginal specula.*

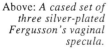

(Left to right) Croft's ebony-handled mouth gag, a steel masticator, for use by edentulous people, and Heister's steel wedge-shaped mouth gag.

other, to which the physician applied his ear. These may be made of wood, ivory, brass or silver. Many modifications to the basic design were made by individual physicians, and many of these eponymous stethoscopes are found today. Very long wooden stethoscopes were used in poorhouses so that the physician could keep his distance from the flea-ridden patient. Some models come apart and in this 'dismounted' form could be carried by the physician in a special silver clip within his top hat! A nineteenth-century catalogue advertises these clips for 'one shilling'. Although the first flexible stethoscope was described in 1851, early tubing was of poor quality and so the rigid monaural types were made well into the twentieth century.

A rare ebony monaural stethoscope, with ivory earpiece, c.1840.

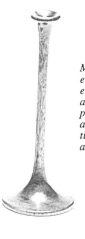

Monaural stethoscopes: (left to right) ebony, with a rubber ring around the earpiece to act as a percussor; ebony; and fruitwood. At the front is a composition instrument showing the 'portable' style. A 1930s catalogue advertises a silver clip for one shilling to fix a portable stethoscope inside a top hat!

Further information about the heart and lungs could be obtained with the technique of percussion. This is now done by tapping one finger on another on the chest wall and listening to the sound produced. In earlier days a percussion hammer was used, and an ivory disc, called a pleximeter, was first held against the wall of the chest and then tapped with the hammer. A rare find is a set combining a percussion hammer and a pleximeter in a fitted case. The best-known is Dr

Bennett's percussor, which has impressions in the ebony handle for the thumb and two fingers.

The first attempts to measure blood pressure were made by Von Basch in 1876, but one of the first instruments to be widely used was the sphygmomanometer, described by Pachon in 1909. Unlike modern sphygmomanometers, this was not used with a stethoscope but used the 'oscillometric' method, by which the blood pressure was determined from the

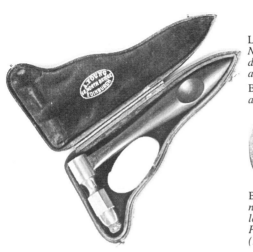

Left: *Dr Bennett's percussor and pleximeter. Note the thumb indentation on the ebony handle. The pleximeter was placed on the chest and tapped with the percussor.*

Below: *A rare ivory pleximeter, with graduation marks and silver handles.*

Below: *Two early blood-pressure devices, both normally within wooden cases with instruction leaflets: (left) Dr Boulitte's oscillometer; (right) Pachon's 'sphygmanometric oscillometer' (1909). Both have pumps, tubing and arm cuffs.*

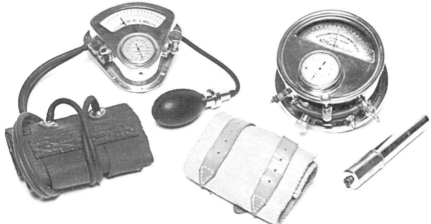

Right: *An early mercury blood-pressure device, Martin's sphygmomanometer, 1920, with one of the first non-spill devices to prevent loss of mercury during movement, and complete with cuff and pump.*

oscillations of the needle on the large dial. Later developments included more accurate measurements with the familiar tube of mercury, and various ingenious 'non-spill' devices to prevent loss of mercury during transport of the instrument.

Sphygmographs were designed from the 1860s to measure and make a permanent recording of the pulse rate and to show the shape of the arterial pulse wave – a valuable clue to certain cardiovascular disorders. Marey's (1860) and Dudgeon's

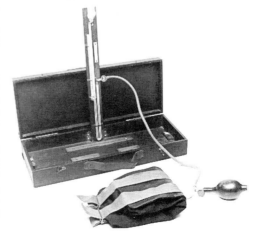

Dudgeon's sphygmograph, 1892, used to record the shape of the pulse wave at the wrist; complete with clockwork for advancing the recording paper, and an ivory dial to adjust the pressure on the artery.

Marey's sphygmograph, invented in 1860 to record the radial artery pulse wave. This example shows a typical record chart on the clockwork-powered carriage. In use the instrument is taped to the wrist.

(1882) sphygmographs are most often seen. Since these instruments were tiresome to set up and use reproducibly, many are in excellent condition, having been very little used.

Ophthalmoscopes have been in use since the late nineteenth century for examining the retina of the eye. Many styles existed, named after their inventors, and including various combinations of mirrors and lenses. Adequate illumination was first achieved using a gas lamp or candle, and May's, Morton's and Liebreich's ophthalmoscopes can all be found, often with ivory handles, for use with an external light source. The collector should always

Two early ophthalmoscopes, by Morton (left) and May. These had to be used, before the days of electric batteries, with a candle or oil lamp to provide illumination.

Immisch's clinical thermometer, one of a range of unusual styles from the late nineteenth century. This was designed in 1881 for measuring skin temperature and was highly acclaimed.

be placed at the back of the 'eye' to mimic disease states. Students could recognise disease patterns and acquire the dexterity needed to manipulate the ophthalmoscope, the lamp and the patient to make accurate diagnoses.

The first clinical thermometer was described in 1684, and one of the earliest that can now be found is described by Currie (1797) in his work on 'Cold water treatment of fevers'. This has a bend of about 30 degrees in its length, so that the scale could easily be read when the bulb was in the armpit. This was important since early thermometers were not 'self-registering', and the mercury began to fall as soon as the thermometer was removed from the patient. Many later nineteenth-century thermometers are contained in attractive boxwood, ivory or silver cases, and two unusual styles include Immisch's clinical thermometer, in the form of a pocket watch, and a skin thermometer, in which the bulb is in the form of a spiral of mercury-filled fine glass tubing.

Another instrument for diagnosis and clinical measurement from the nineteenth century is the dynamometer – a simple spring-loaded device for measuring the strength of the handgrip.

look for instruments complete with their shaped velvet-lined cases. Such instruments will usually be in superior condition and hold their value better. A rare find is Dr Beale's self-illuminating ophthalmoscope with its integral oil lamp and chimney.

Early ophthalmoscopes required considerable training in their use, and in the recognition of diseases in the retina. To help with training, schematic eyes were made of black lacquered metal, with a set of interchangeable painted discs that could

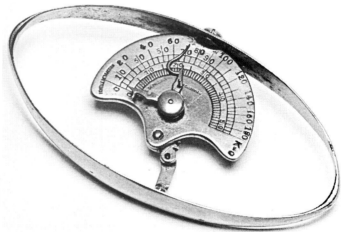

A dynamometer, about 1890, for measuring the strength of the handgrip.

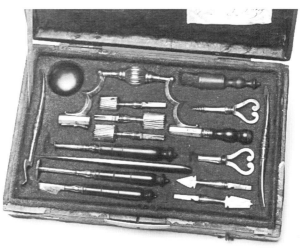

A comprehensive French trepanning set, c.1800, showing a large trepanning brace with three graduated crowns, a bone brush, a raspatory (file) on the right, an elevator on the left, and three ebony-handled lenticulars towards the front. Made by Grangeret, Paris.

SURGICAL INSTRUMENTS

The operation of trephining was known in neolithic times, and the healed edges of wounds in skulls found during archaeological excavations are proof that patients survived the operation, which was carried out using a flint. Surgical saws, knives and forceps were known to the Romans.

The first pictorial evidence of an amputation saw is a painting from 1517, and the collector can find saws from the last two hundred years without much difficulty. Most impressive are the large 'capital' amputation saws, up to 60 cm long, used for removal of limbs, often following severe injury or gangrene on the battlefield.

Iron-framed eighteenth-century saws often have highly decorative features and an elaborate tensioning screw. Saw handles were large, and circular in cross-section until about 1770, when a hexagonal shape was invented to improve grip. Many of the changes to the shape and size of saws reflected designs for special purposes. An elegant little saw, with an 8 cm long fine-toothed blade, was invented by Benjamin Bell in 1780 for amputation of the fingers, and Richard Butcher described his bow saw, with its fine flexible blade designed to minimise injury to soft tissue, in 1851. The fine teeth of many saws easily became clogged with bone dust, and many amputation sets have little bone brushes to remove this.

Many other saws were designed for special purposes, such as Gigli's chain saw, with

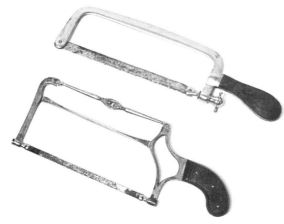

A nineteenth-century capital amputation saw (above) with hatched ebony handle. (Below) Dr Butcher's saw, c.1860, with its fine blade, with tension adjustment, designed to minimise damage to soft tissue during surgery.

10

A chain saw with ebony handles – used when access was difficult.

its two ebony handles. Because of its flexibility it could be used in situations where it was impossible to use a rigid saw. Finger saws with fine narrow blades and ebony or ivory handles are found in most amputation sets, together with skull saws consisting of a short rectangular or semicircular blade at the end of an ebony or ivory handle (Hey's saw).

A trephine is a special saw with a circular cutting edge, frequently tapered slightly so that it does not sink into the brain once the skull has been sawn through. Trephines may be large decorative brace-like instruments or short instruments with a brass stem about 10 cm long and an ebony T-shaped handle. Many trephines have a central sliding pin, used to localise the saw accurately on the skull. Trepanning sets usually contain one or more trephines of differing diameters, a file or raspatory to trim the bone edges, an elevator to assist in removing the bone disc, and one or more lenticulars, which have a sharpened edge to the shaft to trim the edge of the hole, the flat disc at the end of the instrument preventing damage to

the underlying brain.

Surgical knives in Roman times had an ornate bronze handle and a straight iron blade, which in most cases has rusted away. In more recent times, but before the days of anaesthesia, strong assistants were necessary to restrain the patient and many surgeons preferred to use a knife curved on its inner edge, so that a complete circumferential cut through the skin and muscles of a limb could be made in one movement. By the mid nineteenth century most knives were straight, up to 40 cm long, and sharpened along one edge. Catlins were special surgical knives, sharpened along both edges, for dissection between bones. Smaller knives and scalpels, many with handles faced with horn or tortoiseshell which enclose the blade (like a pen or pocket knife), are found in large amputation sets and the smaller 'pocket' sets in leather wallets used to carry out minor procedures in the home.

Short knives with parallel edges were known as bistouries and were designed for dissection of internal organs. Some, with only the terminal 1-2 cm of one edge sharpened, were used for hernia repair and known as hernia bistouries.

The surgical instruments found at Pompeii, and which can now be seen at the National Archaeological Museum at

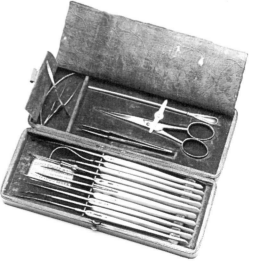

A small surgical set, with scissors, forceps, ear scoop/probe, needles, ten various ivory-handled scalpels and bistouries, a clamp and an aneurysm needle.

Naples, include many pairs of forceps, in various styles, apparently designed for specific purposes. Special forceps for clamping piles and extracting bullets were known in the sixteenth century. The first spring forceps with crossed legs were described by Perret in 1771, and the self-locking forceps for securing arteries against haemorrhage were designed by Charriere in 1840. Military surgical sets occasionally include 'bullet forceps' for removing foreign bodies from wounds, and some trepanning sets include forceps with two semicircular blades for removal of the bone disc.

Surgical scissors are often found in instrument sets and may be indistinguishable from scissors designed for domestic uses. On the whole surgical scissors were more finely made, and many have decorative features, rare examples having silver handles.

removed by the operation of 'cutting for stone' over thousands of years. The most characteristic instruments were those that were inserted into the bladder to locate the stone by touch, then to extract it using the jaws at the end of the instrument. Sometimes it was necessary to crush stones in the bladder before extracting the pieces. The instruments for crushing and extracting stones are lithotrites, and the large number of nineteenth-century instruments available testifies to the high prevalence of stones in the bladder during that period. Other urinary instruments include bladder catheters, often of silver, and in cased sets of graduated size. Some male catheters are telescopic, to fit within pocket instrument sets. A special curved instrument, the bistoury cache, is provided with a concealed sharp blade. It can be placed in the urethra, and the blade opened to cut through a stricture – usually caused

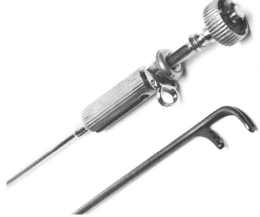

A lithotrite, showing the two ends of this 30 cm long instrument used to crush bladder stones. The closed jaws were passed into the bladder, the stones identified by touch, grasped between the jaws and crushed by closing the jaws. The knurled knob adjusted the jaws.

Other minor surgical instruments used by the family physician included ear scoops for removing wax, probes with rounded ends to search for bullets and other foreign bodies in wounds, and directors, used in hernia repair and other operations. These small instruments are often made of silver, though they may be black through tarnishing.

Many surgical instruments were made for special purposes. Bladder stones were

by venereal disease.

The special instruments for ear, nose and throat surgery include examination sets, with a head mirror, and long-handled instruments to examine the throat. Belloq's nasal cannula is a curved silver catheter containing a spring-loaded probe through which sutures can be threaded, used to snare polyps in the nose.

Many instruments have been designed to remove the tonsils. The most interest-

A cased set of tracheostomy instruments, showing two hooks, a scalpel and three graduated tracheostomy tubes.

teristic autopsy item is a pair of bowel scissors, which have a spike on one blade to stop the bowel slipping out from between the blades during cutting!

Obstetric forceps have been known in Britain since the seventeenth century, and many older styles are named after the obstetrician who invented them. The most attractive have ebony or ivory handles, and sets of instruments may include two or three forceps, perforators, cranioclasts and decapitation hooks. These instruments were sadly necessary when there was no safe way of delivering a live baby and protecting the mother's life when delivery was obstructed. Perforators were used to open the skull, cranioclasts to crush it, and hooks to remove the infant in parts.

A variety of instruments was used to stop bleeding both during surgery and on

ing have a fork for securing the tonsil and a set of knives acting like a guillotine. Small silver tracheostomy tubes can be found in sets of graduated sizes, together with an introducer (like a large-calibre curved trocar) and a small knife. The tubes were used to improve the airway.

Some of the most delicate and beautifully made instruments were used for eye surgery. A typical nineteenth-century ophthalmic surgery set may contain up to thirty ivory-handled knives, probes, hooks and needles, one or more pairs of straight or curved fine scissors, sometimes with silver handles, and retractors to hold the eyelids open.

Some postmortem instruments such as scalpels and scissors differ little, if at all, from their surgical counterparts, but a typical cased set contains a stout saw, a long straight brain knife, a spine wrench and mallet and several tissue hooks. A charac-

A set of ophthalmic instruments in a velvet-lined brass-bound rosewood case. The three scissors have silver handles, and there are 26 various ivory-handled knives, bistouries, hooks and forceps, and a silver ophthalmic syringe.

the battlefield in the eighteenth and nineteenth centuries. One characteristic tourniquet is similar in style to a G clamp. A standard design in the second half of the nineteenth century was Petit's tourniquet, with its brass body and screw, and webbing strap – frequently found in surgical sets.

Discovery of the bacterial origin of infections led to the development of equipment used during surgery to achieve sterility in the wound. Lister-type carbolic sprays were widely used, both in hospitals and by the family doctor, and consist of a small water boiler, heated by a spirit

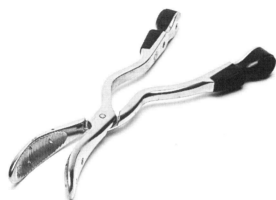

Craniotomy forceps, with ebony handles and spikes within the curved steel blades.

lamp. The jet of steam from the boiler is passed over a beaker of carbolic acid, so spraying the wound with antiseptic vapour.

Anaesthetic apparatus was not produced in large quantities until the last quarter of the nineteenth century, and much of the equipment is not decorative, is incomplete or is very bulky, and only of interest to specialist collectors. Among smaller items regularly found are small ether dropping bottles, with a mechanism to regulate the flow of the anaesthetic on to a gauze mask. Complete self-contained anaesthetic sets may also be found, the most common being Dr Ombredanne's inhaler,

with its decorative brass body, with graduations marking the strength of anaesthetic, and waxed paper inflation bag. It was invented in 1908 and was rumoured to have been used by the Argentinians in the Falklands War, 1982.

Mention must finally be made here of the very decorative cases built to house instrument sets. Many are of mahogany, walnut or rosewood, lined with decorative velvet, and occasionally with the name of the surgeon on the brass cartouche outside the lid. Some collectors derive considerable pleasure from researching the careers of past owners of these sets.

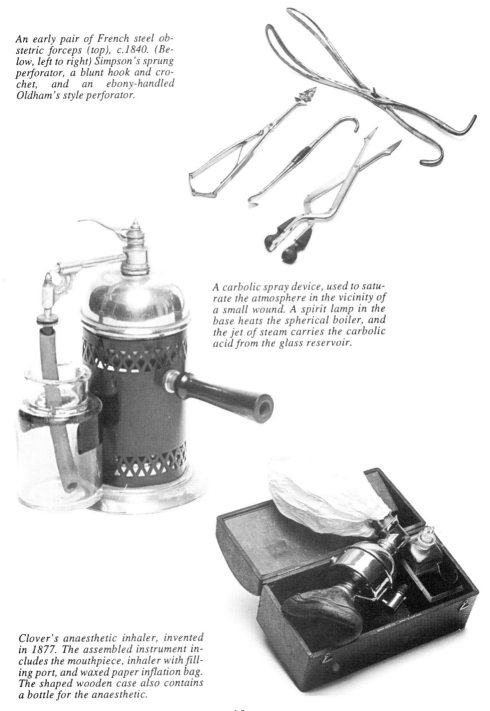

An early pair of French steel obstetric forceps (top), c.1840. (Below, left to right) Simpson's sprung perforator, a blunt hook and crochet, and an ebony-handled Oldham's style perforator.

A carbolic spray device, used to saturate the atmosphere in the vicinity of a small wound. A spirit lamp in the base heats the spherical boiler, and the jet of steam carries the carbolic acid from the glass reservoir.

Clover's anaesthetic inhaler, invented in 1877. The assembled instrument includes the mouthpiece, inhaler with filling port, and waxed paper inflation bag. The shaped wooden case also contains a bottle for the anaesthetic.

Left: *A French faience barber's bowl, with characteristic cut-away crescent.*
Right: *A pewter bleeding bowl, 13 cm in diameter, with rings within at intervals of 4 fluid ounces.*

INSTRUMENTS FOR BLEEDING
AND CUPPING

Bleeding has been an accepted panacea for a wide variety of complaints for centuries and, in the form of cupping, is still used in some less developed parts of Europe.

Bleeding was accomplished by draining blood into a pewter or ceramic bleeding bowl from a puncture wound in a vein. It seems likely that barbers' bowls, with their convenient crescent-shaped cutaway rim, were also used as bleeding bowls, and they are normally considered as 'medical' items. They can form a collecting field in their own right, since they can be made from pewter, tinplate, brass or earthenware, decorated in a wide range of styles.

Steel lancets were used to open veins, and in their most widely available form they consist of a very sharp-pointed steel knife about 4 cm long, housed within tortoiseshell covers when not in use. Lancets were carried in attractive cases made of silver, shagreen, mother-of-pearl or tortoiseshell, and these remain popular collectors' items, often bearing the name of their physician owners.

Other instruments used for bleeding include single-bladed spring lancets, housed in a decorative brass case with a spring mechanism. These are sometimes found in highly attractive leather-covered cases lined with velvet. Many German examples have 'Beware, it pricks' written ornately in Gothic script in gilt on the lid of the case.

Leeches were held by pharmacists and physicians in large decorative ceramic pots, with perforated lids, and Staffordshire leech jars are valued collectors' items. Small stocks of leeches were taken to a patient's home in pewter boxes, about 10 cm long, with a perforated hinged cover at one end. Glass leech tubes, slightly tapered so that the leech was wedged in the narrow end with only its mouth parts protruding, were used to apply leeches within body cavities, such as the mouth. This ensured that the leech was not lost or swallowed during treatment!

Scarificators were used until well into the twentieth century to achieve bleeding. They were first described in the seventeenth century and consist of a brass box, about 5 by 5 by 3 cm, with four to sixteen spring-loaded blades which were released to make a series of short cuts in the skin. Blood was collected in a cupping glass. These were thick-walled vessels, varying in size from an eggcup to a teacup, with a

16

A shagreen-covered lancet case with silver mounts, and four lancets in tortoiseshell covers, also with silver mounts, c.1860.

A small spring lancet, c.1830, in a leather-covered chamois-lined wooden case. The blade is released by pressing the brass lever on top of the instrument.

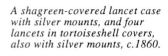

thick rolled rim to achieve an airtight fit on the skin. The glass was first heated with a candle or spirit lamp, then applied over the scarified skin. As the glass cooled, the vacuum drew blood into the glass. Sometimes a syringe was used, with valved cupping glasses, to achieve a vacuum.

Cupping sets, often in attractive mahogany or rosewood cases lined with velvet, therefore contained scarificators, a spirit lamp, a set of glasses and a glass spirit bottle, with or without a brass pump. Collectors should beware of incomplete sets or sets made up from several sources.

Another form of cupping, dry cupping, requires the heated glass to be applied to the skin, which is not first scarified. The glass then draws blood into the skin in the form of a circular bruise.

A rare bleeding device is the mechanical leech. This consists of a glass tube with a plunger, rather like an open-ended syringe. These were sometimes fitted with a scarificator mechanism at the open end and performed as a combined scarificator and cupping glass.

A mahogany-cased cupping set, showing the scarificator (left), a brass syringe and two nests of three cupping glasses, protected by chamois leather.

A rare sterling silver ear trumpet, marked 1812 (left), and a silver-plated trumpet with ebony earpiece and very decorative grille over the void.

HEARING AIDS

The use of the cupped hand or some artificial substitute to improve hearing must have been known to man from earliest times. The first hearing aids were probably cattle horns, the wide end of which could be turned towards the speaker. By the seventeenth century these were sometimes embellished with ivory or silver. Purpose-made ear trumpets can be found from the eighteenth century, the most decorative being of silver or gold, sometimes with elaborate embellishment, and fitted in fishskin cases. A vast range of sizes and styles was made in the nineteenth century, of tinplate, brass, silver and tortoiseshell, sometimes in pairs in decorative cases. One of the largest was 70 cm long, in black japanned tinplate. Many attractive silver-plated trumpets were made by the London firm of F. C. Rein in the 1860s. Trumpets of tinplate and imitation tortoiseshell were made up to the 1930s.

An interesting find is a long conical ear trumpet elaborately decorated with black silk and lace, made to look like a parasol and worn in Victorian times with mourning black.

A rare conversation tube with horn mouthpiece and earpiece, signed Rein, London; 1.5 metres long.

Tiny silver or gold hearing aids designed to be left in the external ear can sometimes be found in pairs, contained in small shaped cases.

Hearing aids in the form of conversation tubes were up to 1.5 metres long, covered in silk, with a long earpiece at one end and a flared mouthpiece at the other.

A small pocket-sized ear trumpet in imitation tortoiseshell, with a telescopic brass ear tube and perforated brass grille; a telescopic banjo-shaped hearing aid (maximum length 32 cm) and a military-issue black japanned ear trumpet with composition earpiece.

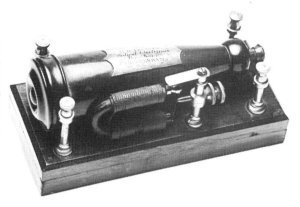

Grigg's conical electro-magnetic machine, dated 8th January 1873. The coil is mounted on a mahogany plinth, together with the brass terminals for connection to wet cell batteries and to the electrodes attached to the patient.

QUACK MEDICINE

Before modern scientific medicine and the regulation of advertising for medical treatments, a large number of proprietary medicines and mechanical devices which were claimed to cure a wide variety of ailments appeared on the market. Such devices could be purchased by the patient, and directions were given for self-use at home. Many of these were electro-galvanic machines, which produced a current either by manual rotation of a coil through a magnetic field or from a set of wet cell batteries. Some have decorative polished brass gearwheels and terminals on polished mahogany or rosewood bases. Current was applied by electrodes, which were either little brass cylinders to be held in the hand, or specially shaped electrodes to be placed on the stomach, feet or back. Many hand-cranked and battery devices are still available and in working order.

A number of medallions were produced in the nineteenth century, made of various metals and claimed to help various musculo-skeletal disorders. These include Boyd's Battery, patented in the United States of America in 1878, and Richardson's Magneto Galvanic Battery, patented in 1891.

Another instrument of uncertain benefit is Baunscheidt's Lebenswecker. This 30 cm long ebony instrument has at its

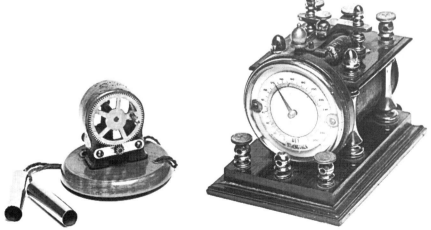

A small hand-cranked galvanic device (left) with two hand electrodes, and a large decorative battery-driven device, with a dial for adjusting the strength of the current.

Baunscheidt's Lebenswecker, made of ebony, with a set of spring-loaded needles for treatment by 'counter-irritation'.

end a series of very sharp pins which can be released into the skin by a spring mechanism. A special oil was first placed at the site, and the process for the relief of symptoms was 'counter-irritation'.

Phrenology is the 'science' of assessing the personality and sensibilities by examining the contours of the skull. Although it is no longer practised, the artefacts associated with phrenology can still be found. They include ceramic phrenology heads from about 1860 marked to show the different areas of the skull. Many are signed 'Fowler' or 'Bridges' but mod-

ern copies can easily confuse the inexperienced collector. Small heads in the form of inkwells and circular snuffboxes embossed with phrenology devices after Dr Gall (1758-1828) are less often found.

Many physical therapy devices of doubtful benefit have been produced from Victorian times, including vibrators and massage instruments. A curiosity still occasionally found is the oculiser, a mechanical device for massaging the (closed) eyes.

Boyd's battery, 3 cm in diameter, consisting of a series of discs made of different metals, and worn to treat various rheumatic complaints. Marked 17th January 1878.

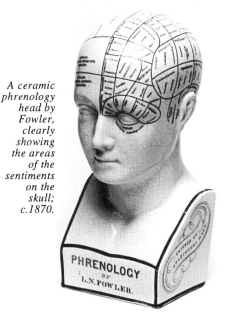

A ceramic phrenology head by Fowler, clearly showing the areas of the sentiments on the skull; c.1870.

Two blue and white ceramic bourdaloues, a rare ceramic spittoon showing the Willow pattern, and a highly decorated Chinese urinal.

DOMESTIC ITEMS

Many objects of interest to collectors of medical items were to be found in Victorian homes. These include equipment associated with infant feeding, breast care and the care of invalids. Silver, pewter and blue and white ceramic pap boats are oval bowls up to 10 cm long, with a lip at one end, used to give semi-solid food to infants. The variety of designs and materials is sufficient to make this a whole collecting field. Baby feeders for dispensing milk include pear-shaped pewter bottles and the more common submarine-shaped feeders, in glass or sometimes highly decorative ceramics. The filling hole on top of these feeders was used to control the flow of milk.

Women who breast-fed babies well after teeth had erupted needed the protection of nipple shields, which may be found in sterling silver, glass, pewter and, rarely, boxwood. Breast pumps could be used to relieve breast engorgement, and some mid-Victorian devices consisted of decorative brass pumps, with a shaped milk reservoir, all stored within a polished velvet-lined mahogany case. Simpler glass versions are still in use.

A wide variety of collectable objects is associated with the care of invalids. Pewter urinals and bedpans from the eight-eenth century onwards are regularly found, as are the more unusual female urinals, called bourdaloues, many of which are highly decorated.

Before the days of antibiotics, and when cigarette smoking, smoke pollution and untreated tuberculosis were common, spitting in public places was normal practice, and various devices were made to deal with the problem indoors. The little blue spitting bottles embossed with name of Dr Dettweiller were made in large numbers and could be carried in the pocket. Elegant spittoons, both ceramic and pewter, were used in the home, and larger versions in hotels and bars.

Several styles of inhaler are frequently found, including the ubiquitous Nelson inhaler, produced in the nineteenth century in attractive decorative styles, and still available in a plain white version. Of more interest is the pewter inhaler described by Mudge in 1778, with its hollow handle, open at the top and bottom, so that air could be warmed by inspiration through hot medicated water. The flexible mouthpiece is usually missing in original examples. Steam kettles were widely used to relieve respiratory symptoms and consisted of a kettle, spirit burner and spout with a jet or other device to

A sterling silver nipple shield, 1835, and a silver pap boat with exterior decora-·tion in the form of a wreath of leaves.

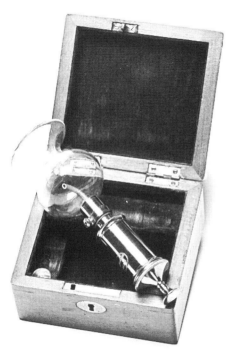

A Mudge-style pewter inhaler. The flexible spout is, as usual, missing from the top. The hollow handle has holes at the top, and at the bottom inside the body of the inhaler, so that air is drawn from the room down through the handle and up through the contained warm liquid.

A mahogany-cased breast pump with brass syringe and characteristic glass trumpet-shaped milk reservoir.

Dr Dettweiller's portable spittoon, embossed with his name, and with a spring-loaded cap and screw-type drainage plug. Several sizes are found, up to 10 cm high.

direct steam to the patient, who sat under a hood or tent.

Spout cups to enable liquids to be given to recumbent patients were known in the seventeenth century, and silver, glass, pewter and ceramic examples are not unusual. Some have the handle and spout at right angles and were designed to be held by the invalid. Silver sick siphons are much rarer. These are hooked to the edge of a cup, and the fine holes at the end of the siphon ensured that the invalid drank fluids only.

In the absence of running water and sanitation the smell in a Victorian sickroom must at times have been unpleasant, and the pastille burner was designed to help deal with the problem. It usually consists of a small ceramic cottage, hollow within, so that an aromatic pastille could be ignited to help disguise the aroma. Spherical brass fumigators, with multiple decorative holes in the hinged upper half of the device, were widely used on the continent for the same purpose and are attractive pieces of 'medical brassware'.

The fly catcher achieved increasing importance in Victorian times once it was recognised that flies might carry disease. It is of clear or coloured glass and has an inner rim, to be filled with sugar water. This attracted flies, which then drowned in it, since they could not find their way out of the apparatus.

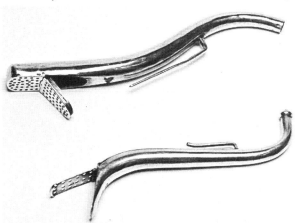

Two silver sick siphons. In use, the hinged foot is closed and the siphon hooked over the lip of a cup so that the invalid can suck only fluid from the cup.

A brass fumigator. The lid of the spherical bowl is perforated and hinged. Aromatic and medicated substances could be placed in the bowl to deal with unpleasant sickroom aromas.

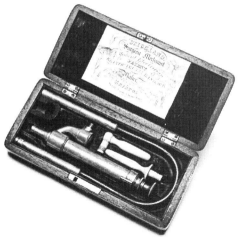

Enemas were widely used in the nineteenth century, and even in the eighteenth century tobacco enemas were used to revive the 'apparently drowned'. Many enema sets are contained in attractive cases, and consist of a brass syringe with brass fittings, a formerly flexible tube and one or more rectal pipes, usually of ivory or pewter. Some cased sets also contain tubes for a stomach pump and for vaginal douching. Certain styles of enema were self-contained, with a large reservoir for fluid, and others needed a separate container for fluid and required the assistance of a family member or other attendant when in use! Very rare are the enema buttons of silvered copper depicting Louis XIV of France enjoying an enema.

Above: *A pewter domestic enema set, showing the syringe, flexible tubing with connectors, and two ivory rectal pipes, all in a mahogany case, 21 cm long; c.1860.*

Right: *Two very rare French enema buttons of Old Sheffield Plate mocking King Louis XIV's predilection for enemas.*

(Left to right) A French douche machine; a large French pewter reservoir-type enema device with integral pipe; and a rare glass reservoir device, with integral brass pump, flexible tubing and pewter pipe.

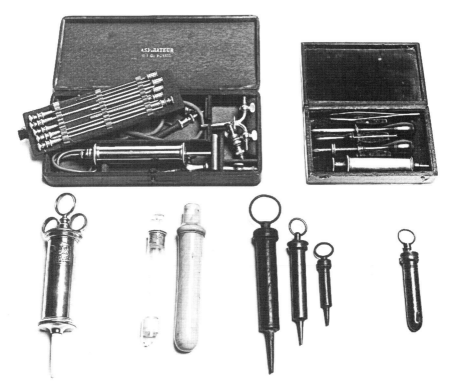

Eight syringes for a variety of purposes: (left to right, top first) Potain's aspiration set, with syringe, three-way tap, tubing and a set of needles for withdrawing fluid from body cavities; a chest aspiration set, with brass syringe, forceps, trocar and cannula, and a second trocar with screw stop to limit the depth of penetration; a brass ear syringe with ivory nozzle; a glass douche syringe and boxwood case; a set of three pewter syringes; and a pewter douche syringe.

TROCARS, CANNULAE AND SYRINGES

One of the most valuable groups of drugs today is the diuretics (water tablets). Before their introduction well into the twentieth century, all large collections of fluid in the body had to be drained mechanically, if at all. A trocar and cannula were used for this purpose. A trocar is a strong sharp steel spike with an ebony or ivory handle. Over the trocar is placed a snugly fitting silver tube, a cannula, open at both ends, and sometimes with holes along its length. The whole assembly was plunged through the wall of the chest or abdomen, the trocar was removed and fluid then flowed out through the cannula. Later syringe sets had the advantage that the syringe could be fitted with a three-way tap and fluid could be actively pumped from the body. A special modification of the trocar and cannula is a Southey's tube set, often consisting of a 3 cm long trocar and an ivory handle which houses up to four delicate silver cannulae. The latter were used to drain fluid from, for example, swollen legs in people with heart failure. The feet would be placed in a bowl to collect the fluid.

A medal commemorating M. F. Xavier Bichat (1771-1802), a French physician and pioneer in scientific histology and pathological anatomy.

MISCELLANEOUS ITEMS

Vaccination was first discovered in the eighteenth century, and a wide variety of instruments was made, many as 'one-offs' for the local doctor. The most widely available collectors' item is a 12 cm long ivory rod with a series of steel spikes at one end, protected when not in use by a silver cover. The other end sometimes contains a silver spatula for applying the serum to the skin.

There are few decorative items in the X-ray field, but early twentieth-century glass X-ray plates are of special interest to physicians, since they illustrate the advanced stages of diseases rarely seen today. Early X-ray tubes are also widely available.

Coins, tokens and medals with medical associations may need to be sought out among boxes of miscellaneous coins in collectors' markets. Many medals were made from the eighteenth century onwards to celebrate a physician, a new hospital, or, more recently, an international symposium. Tokens were issued by chemists and manufacturers of proprietary medicines and could be exchanged for goods.

There is a special pleasure in handling items that are two thousand or more years old, and several antiquities with medical significance are not difficult to find. Amulets, small charms worn to bring good fortune, healing of disease or increased fertility, are found in the form of many body parts and usually have holes for attaching them to a necklace or to clothing.

A terracotta Roman feeder, with black slip, 7 cm high.

Spouted terracotta vessels about 5 cm high, and containing milk residues, have been found in the tombs of children and are thought by some to be baby feeders. Small bronze spatulas, tweezers, probes and other instruments may have had uses in medicine, pharmacy or cosmetics. Rarely, bronze surgical instrument handles are found, the iron blades having rusted away.

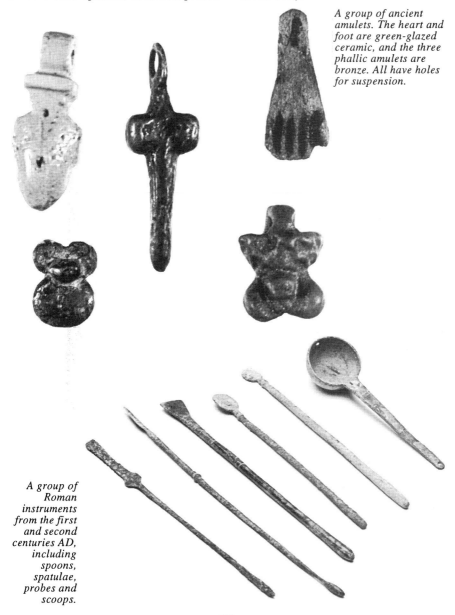

A group of ancient amulets. The heart and foot are green-glazed ceramic, and the three phallic amulets are bronze. All have holes for suspension.

A group of Roman instruments from the first and second centuries AD, including spoons, spatulae, probes and scoops.

27

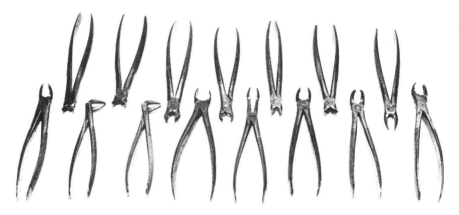

A group of fifteen steel dental forceps, showing a variety of styles to deal with different teeth, and some for extraction of roots.

DENTAL INSTRUMENTS

Teeth have been extracted since ancient times, and accounts from the twelfth century describe the head of the patient held between the knees of the operator, and a red-hot cautery iron being applied to the gum to stop bleeding! For many years extraction was the only available dental remedy.

Early extractions were probably carried out using blacksmith's tools. The first purpose-made instrument for this operation was the pelican – now a rare and expensive find. Although it was first described in the fourteenth century, most examples available to the collector date from the nineteenth and twentieth centuries. Early examples are all steel and have a single bolster with a rotating hook, with a gap of about 6 mm between them. The tooth was prised out sideways, the crown being grasped between the hook and the bolster. Later examples had a screw mechanism to adjust the width to the tooth to be extracted, and some have ebony or ivory handles.

Toothkeys for extractions were first used in the eighteenth century, and consisted of an ebony, ivory or horn

handle, and a 13 cm long steel shaft bearing a semicircular hook. The key was hooked at the root of the tooth, and extraction achieved by forceful upward movement. Teeth were often broken as a result, and ebony-handled elevators and steel forceps were used to remove remaining fragments. To reduce the chance of breaking the jaw at the same time as extracting teeth, toothkeys had a double bend introduced into the shaft to give it a U shape. Many nineteenth-century toothkeys are designed this way.

Dental forceps were described by Albucasis, and there have been many styles in the subsequent centuries, some in the form of combination instruments, with integral hooks or elevators. Early iron examples may be very decorative, as are the very rare examples with ebony handles. Many later examples are marked with the name of the tooth they were de-

An eighteenth-century pelican, with ebony handle and a screw mechanism to adjust the gap between the bolster and the claw.

28

Three toothkeys with ebony handles and double bends to the shaft; one has a double claw.

signed to extract.

Small dental mirrors can occasionally be found, and they may be very attractive, with decorative ivory or silver handles.

A wide range of probes and pluggers for conservative dentistry is available, and the most decorative are in sets with ivory or ebony handles, sometimes fitted in velvet-lined cases.

The most desirable dental collectors' pieces are sets of instruments, containing toothkeys, forceps, hygiene instruments, dental mirrors and, rarely, a pelican. These sets may be in very attractive cases, lined with velvet, and now command very high prices.

Cast-iron foot drills for use in conservative dentistry regularly appear in country auctions, being virtually indestructible. More interesting are the small hand-held ivory-handled drills. Some of these used the Archimedean screw principle, and their slow speed must have required considerable fortitude on the part of the patient!

By the eighteenth century dental hygiene sets were introduced. These attractive items typically contain up to six small tools with a common ivory handle, all fitted into a fishskin case, with a

Five dental elevators for assisting in tooth extraction and in the removal of remnants left after incomplete extraction. All with ebony handles.

mirror within the lid. The teeth could be kept clean by regular scraping and poking. These sets are decorative collectors' pieces, available in a wide range of styles, and take very little room. Other hygiene implements include tongue scrapers, made in a wide range of materials, and toothpicks, most commonly in the form of a small silver blade which retracts into a silver sheath.

Many dental models were made for teaching purposes. These may be elaborate and anatomically correct wax or papier-mâché models, or meticulous dissections of human jaws, showing the teeth and the blood vessels and nerves supplying them. Heavy dental models showing various reconstructive techniques occasionally appear in specialist dealers' catalogues. Many are beautifully made and demonstrate gold teeth, bridges and other

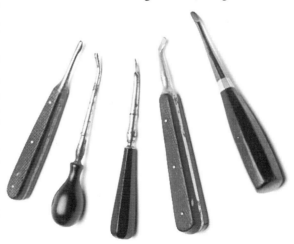

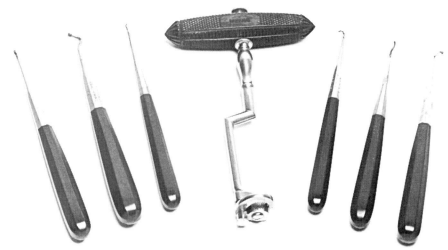

A group of six probes and pluggers for conservative dentistry, with an ebony-handled toothkey, all c.1880.

dental replacement techniques, especially those from Wenkabe.

Dental chairs and other items of specialised dental furniture occasionally appear for sale, and it is sometimes possible to purchase the contents of early dental surgeries in their entirety. These require a large amount of space, but some collectors gain considerable pleasure from assembling over a period of several years, a complete set of furniture, instruments and accessories from a specific era. Catalogues of dental instruments and equipment are invaluable in planning such a project, since they show which items are contemporary with one another.

Many single instruments are not very decorative, and for display purposes the collector may wish to concentrate on cased sets. The boxes are often lined with attractive velvet and silk and may contain instruments for extraction or the attractive groups of ivory-handled instruments for dental hygiene.

Left: An early nineteenth-century dental hygiene set, with six implements and a common ivory handle. Many sets have a small mirror in the lid.

Right: A group of tongue scrapers made (left to right) from tortoiseshell and ivory, silver and silver and ivory.

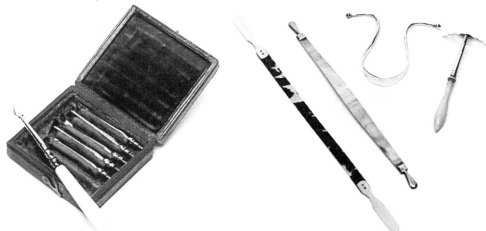

FURTHER READING

Bennion, Elisabeth. *Antique Medical Instruments.* Philip Wilson Publishers Ltd for Sotheby Parke Bernet Publications, 1979.

Bennion, Elisabeth. *Antique Dental Instruments.* Philip Wilson Publishers Ltd for Sotheby's Publications, 1986.

Bennion, Elisabeth. *Antique Hearing Devices.* Vernier Press, 1994.

Carter, Bill; Butterworth, Bernard; Carter, Joseph; and Carter, John. *Dental Collectibles and Antiques.* Dental Folklore Books, Kansas City, Missouri, USA, 1984.

Corson, Richard Owen. *Fashions in Eyeglasses.* Peter Owen, 1980.

Crellin, J. K. *Medical Ceramics,* volume 1. Wellcome Institute of the History of Medicine, 1969.

Crellin, J. K., and Scott, J. R. *Glass and British Pharmacy, 1600 to 1900.* Wellcome Institute of the History of Medicine, 1972.

Damman, Gordon. *Pictorial Encyclopedia of Civil War Medical Instruments and Equipment.* Pictorial Histories Publishing Company, Missoula, Montana, 1983.

Davis, Audrey B. *Medicine and Its Technology.* Greenwood Press, 1981.

Davis, Audrey, and Appel, Toby. *Bloodletting Instruments in the National Museum of History and Technology.* The Printers Devil, 1983.

Fredgant, D. *Medical, Dental and Pharmaceutical Collectibles.* Books Americana, 1981.

Hamarneh, S. K., and Stieb, E. W. *Pharmacy Museums and Historical Collections on Public View in the United States and Canada.* The National Museum of American History, 1981.

Hoffmann-Axthelm, W. *History of Dentistry.* Quintessence Publishing Company, 1981.

Matthews, L. G. *Antiques of the Pharmacy.* G. Bell and Sons, 1971.

Milne, J. S. *Surgical Instruments in Greek and Roman Times.* Augustus M. Kelley, 1970.

Spink, M. S., and Lewis, G. L. *Albucasis on Surgery and Instruments.* Wellcome Institute of the History of Medicine, 1973.

Thomas, K. B. *The Development of Anaesthetic Apparatus.* Blackwell Scientific Publications, 1975.

Turner, G. L'E. *Antique Scientific Instruments.* Blandford Press, 1980.

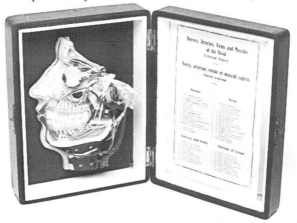

A German wax model of the head and neck to show the detailed anatomy and the blood and nerve supply to the teeth.

PLACES TO VISIT

Intending visitors are advised to find out the hours of opening and whether relevant items are on display before making a special journey.

UNITED KINGDOM

British Dental Association Museum, 64 Wimpole Street, London W1M 8AL. Telephone: 0171 935 0875. (By appointment only.) Website: www.bda-dentistry.org.uk

Cambridge and County Folk Museum, 2/3 Castle Street, Cambridge CB3 0AQ. Telephone: 01223 355159.

Hall's Croft (The Shakespeare Birthplace Trust), Old Town, Stratford-upon-Avon, Warwickshire CV37 6BG. Telephone: 01789 292107.

Ironbridge Gorge Museum Trust, Ironbridge, Telford, Shropshire TF8 7AW. Telephone: 01952 433522. Website: www.vtel.co.uk/igmt

Monica Britton Memorial Hall, Postgraduate Medical Education Centre, Frenchay Hospital, Bristol BS16 1LE. Telephone: 0117 975 3704.

Museum of the History of Science, Broad Street, Oxford OX1 3AZ. Telephone: 01865 277280. Website: www.ashmol.ox.ac.uk

Museum of the Wellcome Institute of the History of Medicine, Science Museum, Exhibition Road, South Kensington, London SW7 2DD. Telephone: 0171 938 8000. Website: www.nmsi.ac.uk

The Old Operating Theatre, Museum and Herb Garret, 9A St Thomas Street, London SE1 9RY. Telephone: 0171 955 4791 or 0181 806 4325. Website: www.southwark.gov.uk/tourism/attractions/old_operating_theatre/index.htm

Royal College of Surgeons of England, 35-43 Lincoln's Inn Fields, London WC2A 3PN. Telephone: 0171 405 3474. Website: www.rcseng.ac.uk

The Shugborough Estate (Staffordshire County Museum), Milford, Stafford ST17 0XB. Telephone: 01889 881388. Website: www.staffordshire.gov.uk/shugboro/shugpark.htm

The Thackray Medical Museum, Beckett Street, Leeds, West Yorkshire LS9 7LN. Telephone: 0113 244 4343.

Ulster American Folk Park, Mellon Road, Castletown, Omagh, County Tyrone, Northern Ireland BT78 5QY. Telephone: 01662 24 3292. Website: www.folkpark.com

Winchester City Museum, The Square, Winchester, Hampshire. Telephone: 01962 848269. Website: www.winchester.gov.uk

Worcester City Museum and Art Gallery, Foregate Street, Worcester WR1 1DT. Telephone: 01905 25371.

York Castle Museum, Eye of York, York YO1 9RY. Telephone: 01904 613161. Website: www.york.gov.uk/heritage/museums/castle

UNITED STATES OF AMERICA

Fort Worth Museum of Science and History, 1501 Montgomery Street, Fort Worth, Texas 76107.

The National Museum of American History, Division of Medical Sciences, Smithsonian Institution, Washington, DC 20560.